MEET THE COMMUNITY HELPERS!

A DAY WITH A LIFEGUARD

FIRST AID KIT

GRASSHOPPER

by Mari Schuh
illustrated by Dean Gray

Ideas for Parents & Teachers

Grasshopper Books introduce children to fiction at the earliest levels. Fun storylines and easy-to-follow text support early readers as they learn to read informational fiction and enhance their imagination. Sight words, repetitive sentence patterns, and fun illustrations support early readers.

Before Reading

- Discuss the cover illustration. What do they see?
- Look at the picture glossary together. Discuss the words.

Read the Book

- Read the book to the child, or have him or her read independently.
- "Walk" through the book and look at the illustrations. Who is the main character? What is happening in the story?

After Reading

- Prompt the child to think more. Ask: Would you like to be a lifeguard? Why or why not?

Grasshopper Books are published by Jump!
5357 Penn Avenue South
Minneapolis, MN 55419
www.jumplibrary.com

Library of Congress Cataloging-in-Publication Data

Names: Schuh, Mari C., 1975– author. | Gray, Dean, illustrator.
Title: A day with a lifeguard / by Mari Schuh; [illustrated by Dean Gray].
Description: Minneapolis, MN: Jump!, Inc., 2025.
Series: Meet the community helpers! | Includes index.
Audience: Ages 5–8
Identifiers: LCCN 2023046306 (print)
LCCN 2023046307 (ebook)
ISBN 9798892130929 (hardcover)
ISBN 9798892130936 (paperback)
ISBN 9798892130943 (ebook)
Subjects: LCSH: Lifeguards—Juvenile fiction.
Readers (Primary) LCGFT: Readers (Publications).
Classification: LCC PE1119.2 .S3729 2025 (print)
LCC PE1119.2 (ebook)
DDC 428.6/2—dc23/eng/20231017
LC record available at https://lccn.loc.gov/2023046306
LC ebook record available at https://lccn.loc.gov/2023046307

Editor: Jenna Gleisner
Direction and Layout: Emma Almgren-Bersie
Illustrator: Dean Gray

Printed in the United States of America at Corporate Graphics in North Mankato, Minnesota.

Table of Contents

Keeping Swimmers Safe

Luis is a lifeguard.

He gets to work early.

Luis tests the pool's water.

It has enough chlorine.

It is safe for swimmers!

It is a busy day at the pool.

Luis makes sure swimmers follow the rules.

"Please walk. Don't run!" he says.

Luis watches the swimmers.

Dana does, too.

They make sure everyone is safe.

CPR
GUARD

Kay teaches swim lessons.

She shows kids how to swim safely.

GUARD

Bo works at the water park.

He helps swimmers go
down the slide.

"One at a time!" he says.

Meg works at the beach.

She watches with binoculars.

A swimmer is in trouble!

Meg runs to help.

Splash!

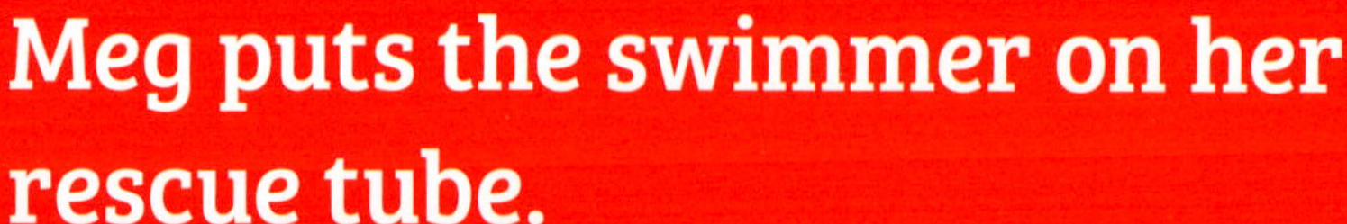

Meg puts the swimmer on her rescue tube.

She brings her safely to shore.

GUARD

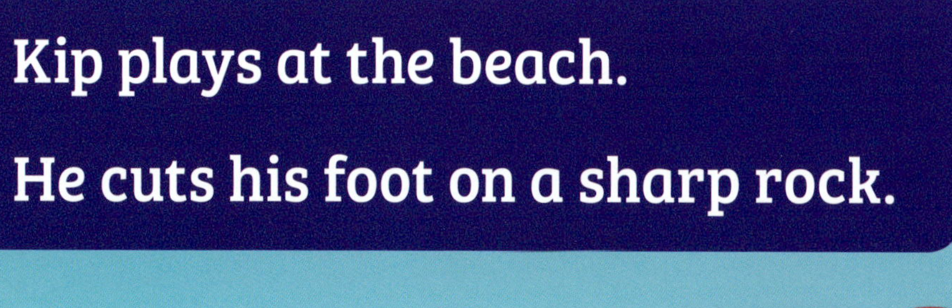

Kip plays at the beach.

He cuts his foot on a sharp rock.

Jon can help!

He cleans the cut and puts a bandage on it.

Lexi blows her whistle.

“Break time! Time to get out of the water,” she says.

Swimmers rest.

So do the lifeguards!

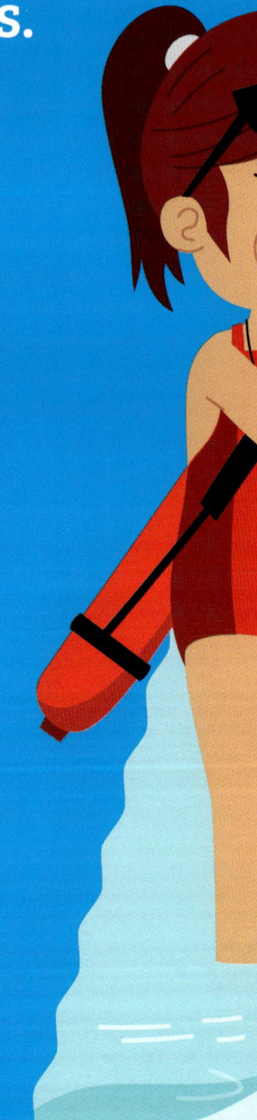

Quiz Time!

What did lifeguard Meg use to help the swimmer at the beach?

A. rescue ring **B.** rescue tube
C. whistle **D.** first aid kit

Lifeguard Tools

Take a look at some of a lifeguard's tools!

Quiz Time! Answer Key: **B.** rescue tube

Picture Glossary

binoculars

A device you look through with both eyes to make things that are far away look larger and closer.

chlorine

A chemical that is added to water to kill bacteria.

rescue tube

A long, strong piece of equipment that floats and is used to rescue swimmers.

swim lessons

Lessons or classes during which people are taught to swim.

Index

To Learn More

Finding more information is as easy as 1, 2, 3.

1. Go to www.factsurfer.com
2. Enter "**adaywithalifeguard**" into the search box.
3. Choose your book to see a list of websites.